KEY STAGE 2   Y3-4

Look you! Look me!

Jacqueline Dineen

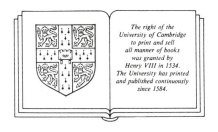

Cambridge University Press

Cambridge   New York   Port Chester   Melbourne   Sydney

Published by the Press Syndicate of the
University of Cambridge
The Pitt Building, Trumpington Street,
Cambridge CB2 1RP
40 West 20th Street, New York,
NY 10011-4211, USA
10 Stamford Road, Oakleigh,
Melbourne 3166, Australia

© Cambridge University Press 1991

First published 1991

Designed by Pardoe Blacker Publishing Ltd,
Shawlands Court, Newchapel Road, Lingfield,
Surrey RH7 6BL
Illustrated by Chris Forsey, Dawn Brend and
Terry Burton
Printed in Great Britain at the University Press,
Cambridge

British Library cataloguing-in-publication data
Dineen, Jacqueline
Look you! Look me!
1. Man. Physiology
I. Title II. Series
612

ISBN 0 521 39753 7

Photographic credits

t=top b=bottom c=centre l=left r=right

Cover: Jenny Woodcock/Bubbles

4l Trevor Hill; 4tr Metropolitan Police Press Library; 4br Peter Aprahamian/Science Photo Library; 5 Trevor Hill; 10 Gray Mortimore/Allsport; 13 Simon Bruty/Allsport; 21 Split Second; 23 Blair Seitz/Science Photo Library; 25 Trevor Hill; 29 Michel Fauquet/Allsport; 33t The Hutchison Library; 33c CNRI/Science Photo Library; 33b St Mary's Hospital Medical School/Science Photo Library; 35 James Holmes/Farmer Giles Foods/Science Photo Library; 37 National Medical Slide Bank; 38t Leo Mason/Split Second; 38bl Trevor Hill; 38br ZEFA; 46 Allsport; 48l Francis Leroy, Biocosmos/Science Photo Library; 48r Andy Walker, Midland Fertility Services/Science Photo Library; 50 Dominique v. Rossum/Petit Format; 52 Jonathan Watts/Science Photo Library; 53 Sally and Richard Greenhill; 55 Trevor Hill; 57 John Howard/Science Photo Library; 59, 60 Trevor Hill.

NOTICE TO TEACHERS
The contents of this book are in the copyright of Cambridge University Press. Unauthorised copying of any of the pages is not only illegal but also goes against the interests of the author.
For authorised copying please check that your school has a licence (through the Local Education Authority) from the Copyright Licensing Agency which enables you to copy small parts of the text in limited numbers.

Contents

Introduction	4	Looking after your body	40
Your skeleton	8	Rest and relaxation	44
How you move	12	The human cycle	46
Breathing and talking	14	A new life	48
Your heart and blood	16	The baby is born	52
What happens to your food?	18	Who do you look like?	54
Your senses	20	A baby's first year	56
Your skin and hair	26	Learning about the world	58
Natural reactions	28	The child grows up	60
Staying healthy	30	Key words	62
A healthy diet	34	Index	64
Taking exercise	38		

Introduction

Think of all the living things on the Earth. You are a living thing. There are all sorts of plants and animals. Birds, fish, insects, **mammals** and **reptiles** are all animals.

Where do you fit in?

You are a mammal. A mammal is a warm-blooded animal with hair or fur on its body to keep it warm. The **temperature** of a mammal's body normally stays the same.

Did you know...?

There are about 4000 types of mammal. They live all over the world, from the poles to the equator.

Most baby mammals grow inside the mother's body until they are born. Then, baby mammals have to be looked after. The mother produces milk to feed them.

Find the difference

Can you think of things that make you different from other mammals? The pictures below will give you some clues.

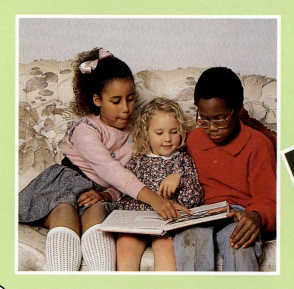

Your brain

Your brain is different from the brains of other mammals. People use their brains to invent things to make life easier or more comfortable. They can solve problems and cure **disease**. People use language to talk to each other. There are about 3000 different languages spoken in the world!

Who do you look like?

Do you look like anyone in your family? Do you look *exactly* the same as them? You may have eyes like one person and hair like another. We will see why later in this book.

Where you come from also makes a difference to how you look. People who come from hotter parts of the world have darker skins than people who come from cooler places.

Even identical twins do not look *exactly* the same. Look at the picture carefully. Can you see any differences?

More about: mammals and other living things – see Life around us
(another *New Horizons* book)

How does your body work?

Your body has many special parts called **organs**. Your heart is an organ, so are your liver, kidneys, eyes and ears. Each of your organs does a special job. Your body works all the time, even when you are asleep. You do not have to think about some of the things it is doing.

1 brain
sends and receives messages which control everything your body does

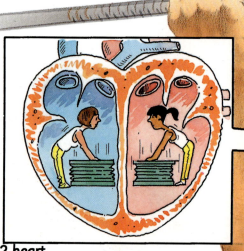

2 heart
pumps blood round your body

3 bones
keep your body upright and protect organs

What your body needs

Food – your **fuel**, just as petrol is a car's fuel.
Oxygen – a **gas** in the air you breathe.

food + oxygen → energy

You need energy to work and keep warm.
Clothes and shelter – to keep warm and dry because you are covered only with fine hairs.

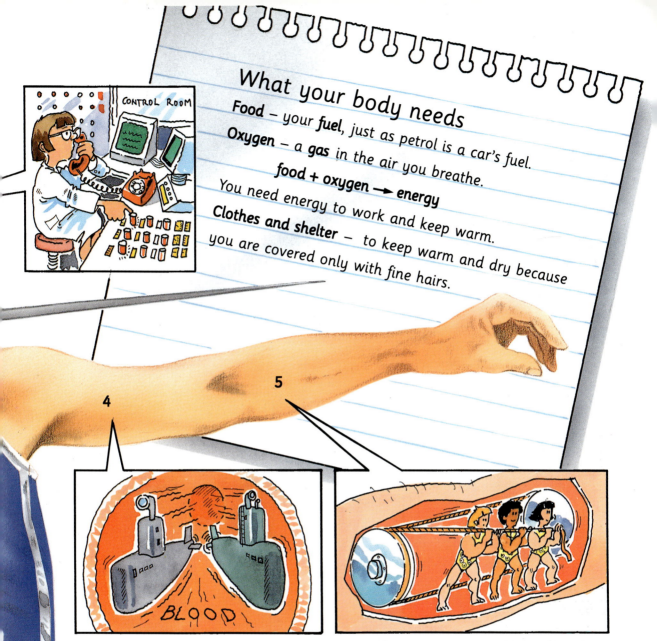

4 blood
  carries oxygen and food to every part of you

5 muscles
  work your bones to let you move

6 liver
  sorts the food and prepares it for your body to use

7 kidneys
  help to clean your blood

More about: bones pp8–9 heart pp16–17 muscles pp12–13

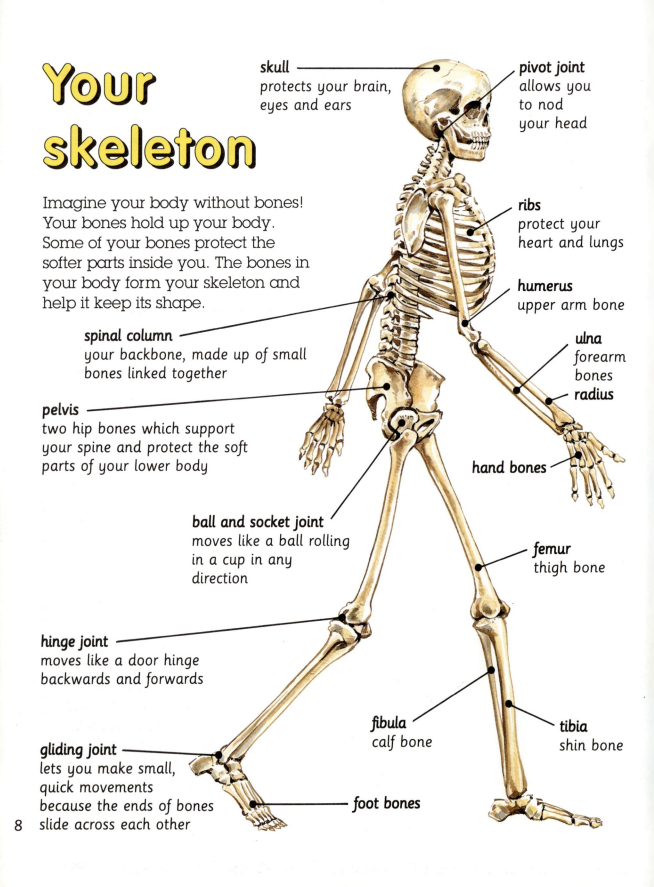

Your skeleton

Imagine your body without bones! Your bones hold up your body. Some of your bones protect the softer parts inside you. The bones in your body form your skeleton and help it keep its shape.

skull — protects your brain, eyes and ears

pivot joint allows you to nod your head

ribs protect your heart and lungs

humerus upper arm bone

ulna forearm bones
radius

spinal column — your backbone, made up of small bones linked together

pelvis — two hip bones which support your spine and protect the soft parts of your lower body

hand bones

ball and socket joint moves like a ball rolling in a cup in any direction

femur thigh bone

hinge joint — moves like a door hinge backwards and forwards

fibula calf bone

tibia shin bone

gliding joint — lets you make small, quick movements because the ends of bones slide across each other

foot bones

What is bone?

Bones do not look alive, but they are! Bones need food to grow. Blood carries food to your bones. When you were a baby, your bones were small and soft. They become harder as you grow.

Did you know...?

- There are more than 200 bones in your skeleton.
- The largest bone is the femur. It is 50 cm long in a person who is 1·8 m tall.
- The smallest bone is the stirrup inside the ear. It is 2·5 mm long.

Inside your bones

Imagine how heavy your bones would be if they were solid! The outside of the bone is hard but the inside looks like sponge.

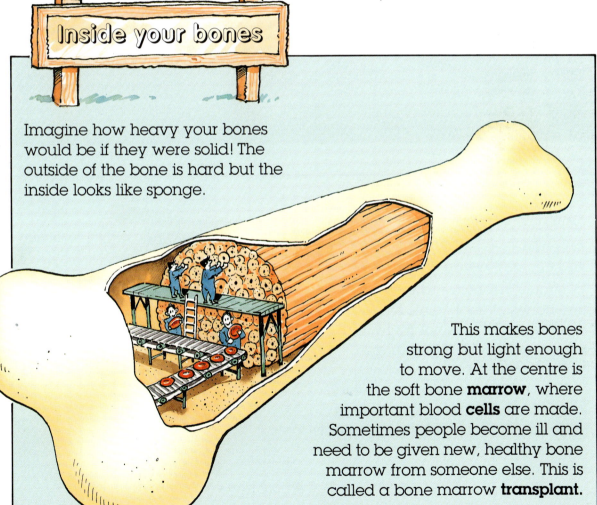

This makes bones strong but light enough to move. At the centre is the soft bone **marrow**, where important blood **cells** are made. Sometimes people become ill and need to be given new, healthy bone marrow from someone else. This is called a bone marrow **transplant**.

More about: blood cells p17   lungs pp14–15   movement pp12–13

Joining your bones together

Bone is too hard to bend but you can bend your body. You can move because there are joints between your bones.

Protecting your joints

Tough bands called **ligaments** hold your joints in place. There is a pad of strong, rubbery material between the bones of each joint. This is called **cartilage**. If it was not there, the bones would rub together and wear away.

Your body makes a liquid which helps the joints move smoothly. It acts like oil in a machine. It protects the moving parts.

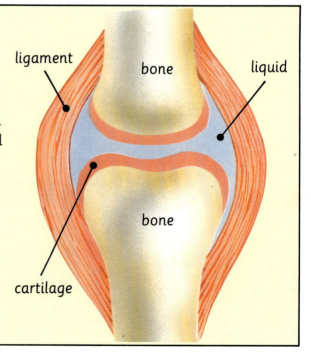

How you move

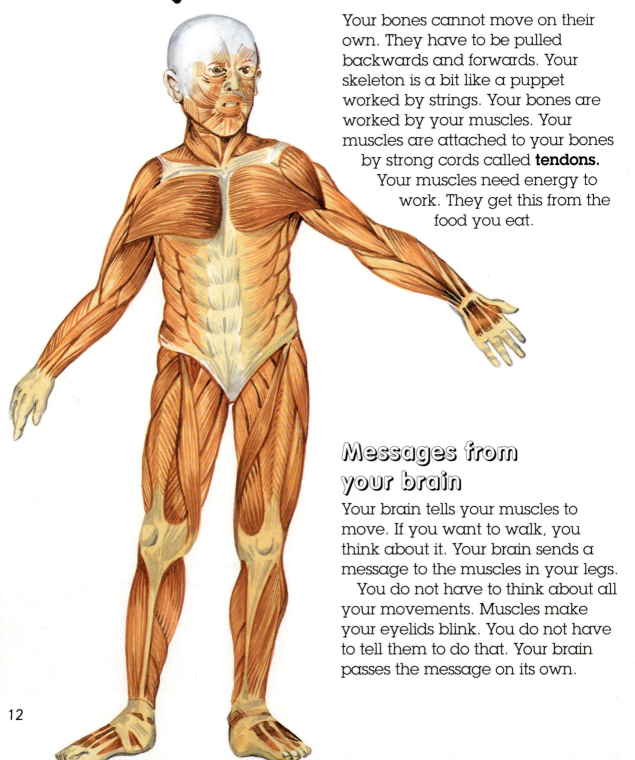

Your bones cannot move on their own. They have to be pulled backwards and forwards. Your skeleton is a bit like a puppet worked by strings. Your bones are worked by your muscles. Your muscles are attached to your bones by strong cords called **tendons.** Your muscles need energy to work. They get this from the food you eat.

Messages from your brain

Your brain tells your muscles to move. If you want to walk, you think about it. Your brain sends a message to the muscles in your legs.

You do not have to think about all your movements. Muscles make your eyelids blink. You do not have to tell them to do that. Your brain passes the message on its own.

Did you know...?
There are about 650 muscles in your body.

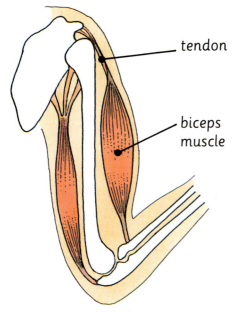

Muscles work in pairs to move your bones. One muscle pulls your arm to make it bend. The other pulls it straight again.

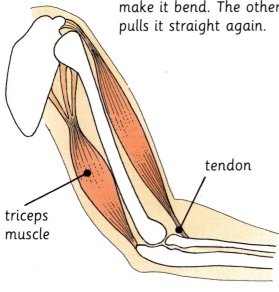

Aches and pains

Sometimes after exercise, your muscles ache, especially if you are not fit! It is best to exercise often so your muscles get used to it.

People can strain or tear muscles. This is called a **sprain**. The sprained muscles have to be bandaged tightly until they heal.

If your muscles suddenly get cold or are strained, they tighten and you may get **cramp**. People sometimes get stomach cramp when they are swimming, especially if they have just eaten. Their stomach muscles have too much to do all at once and become strained.

Have you ever had a stitch? When the muscles run out of energy, they produce a special liquid which causes a sharp pain. It goes away if you stop to rest.

A sudden strain has given this footballer cramp in his leg muscles.

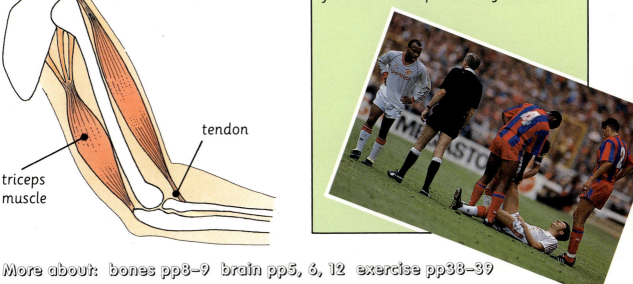

More about: bones pp8–9   brain pp5, 6, 12   exercise pp38–39

Breathing and talking

Put your hands on your ribs and breathe deeply. Can you feel them going in and out?

You breathe all the time, even when you are asleep. You breathe in and out without thinking about it.

What happens to the air you breathe?

tiny hairs inside your nose trap bits of dust and dirt

your ribs protect your lungs

air travels down your windpipe into your lungs

your lungs are like two stretchy, spongy bags

The oxygen your body needs passes from your lungs into your blood.

Your body produces another gas called **carbon dioxide**.

Carbon dioxide travels in your blood back to your lungs. You get rid of it when you breathe out.

As you breathe in, your lungs fill with air like balloons. As you breathe out, they empty.

When you breathe in:

strong muscles move your ribs up and out to make room for the air

air rushes into your lungs

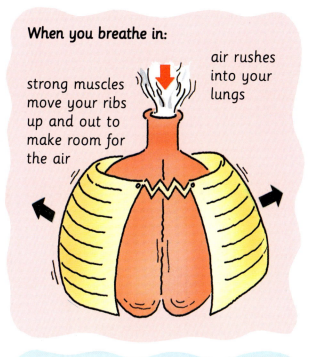

When you exercise, your muscles need more energy to keep going and so you breathe faster.

How you talk

At the top of your **windpipe** you have a voice box. Inside are two flat bands called **vocal cords.** When you breathe out, air passes through a small gap between them. They move or **vibrate**, making sound. Humans make special sounds called speech. We speak by forming words with our lips and tongue.

Voice box

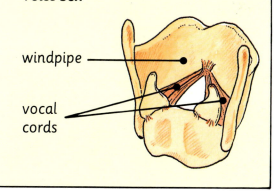

windpipe

vocal cords

When you breathe out:

ribs are pulled in and push against your lungs

air is squeezed out

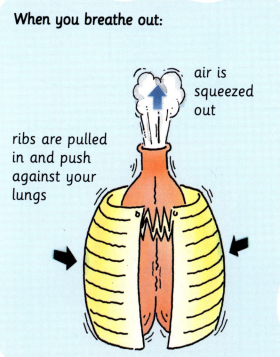

When you are out playing, try to use your voice to make a loud sound. What did you have to do?

More about: blood pp16–17 lungs pp17, 39 muscles pp12–13

Your heart and blood

If you cut any part of your body, you bleed. But you are not just a bag filled with blood! Your heart is made of strong muscle. When it beats, it pumps your blood around your body through long tubes.

Your delivery service

➡ Blood can flow only one way.

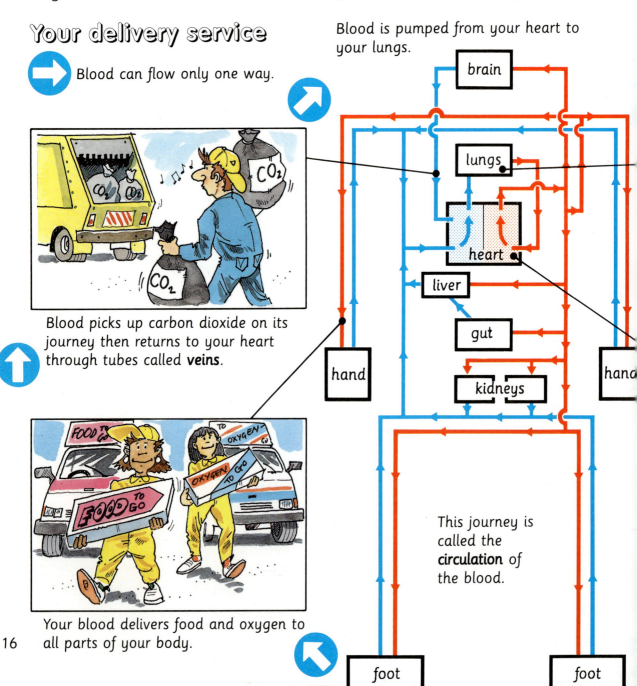

Blood picks up carbon dioxide on its journey then returns to your heart through tubes called **veins**.

Blood is pumped from your heart to your lungs.

Your blood delivers food and oxygen to all parts of your body.

This journey is called the **circulation** of the blood.

What is blood?

Blood contains millions of cells. Most are red blood cells which carry oxygen around your body. There are also white blood cells which attack **germs** and destroy them.

Germs are all around us. They are so small that you cannot see them. If they get into your body they can cause illness.

In your lungs blood collects oxygen from the air you breathe and gets rid of carbon dioxide.

Blood flows back to your heart.

Your heart pumps blood around your body through tubes called **arteries**.

How a wound heals

When you cut yourself, you bleed. When the blood meets the air, it gets thicker and **clots**. It spreads over the cut and forms a scab to stop more blood flowing out.

The scab stops dirt getting into the cut. New skin grows under the scab. Then, the scab falls off.

Sometimes you bump part of your body but the skin is not cut. The blood collects underneath and makes a bruise.

Put your hand over your heart. Can you feel it beat? It should beat about 70 times a minute. How many times will it beat in an hour? In 24 hours?

Did you know...?

Your blood takes about half a minute to go right round your body. Your heart pumps your blood round your body more than 2800 times a day!

More about: breathing pp14–15 heart p6 lungs pp14, 15, 38, 39

What happens to your food?

In your mouth you chew food. Your teeth grind the food into bits.

The watery liquid in your mouth is called **saliva**. It mixes with the food and softens it.

Your body needs food to give it energy. You also need food to grow. Parts of your body are growing and changing all the time.

Many things have to happen to food before your body can use it for energy. This is called **digestion**.

Solid waste is pushed out of your body by strong muscles.

Liquid waste is trapped by your two kidneys. You get rid of this in your **urine**. Urine collects in a stretchy bag called the **bladder**. What happens when your bladder is full?

solid waste

large intestine

Your senses

Your senses are hearing, sight, touch, taste and smell. They tell you what is going on around you. They send information to your brain along special pathways called **nerves** from every part of you.

Your brain is like a computer. It stores information. When you first met your friends, your eyes told you what they looked like. Your ears heard their names. Your eyes and ears passed messages to your brain. It stored them away. Now when you see your friends, you recognise them and remember their names.

Hearing

How the ear works

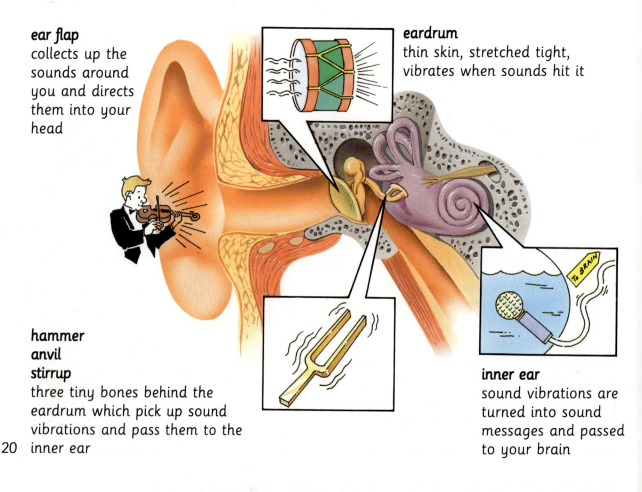

ear flap
collects up the sounds around you and directs them into your head

eardrum
thin skin, stretched tight, vibrates when sounds hit it

hammer
anvil
stirrup
three tiny bones behind the eardrum which pick up sound vibrations and pass them to the inner ear

inner ear
sound vibrations are turned into sound messages and passed to your brain

> Never push anything into your ears. They are delicate and can be damaged easily.

Why do you get dizzy?

Look at the picture of the ear. Can you see three tubes shaped like loops? They are filled with liquid.

As the liquid moves, messages go to your brain. They tell it whether you are standing up, lying down, or turning your head. When you spin fast, the liquid swirls round. Your brain gets confused and cannot control your balance properly.

Why doesn't this skater fall over? She has practised spinning round and round and her brain is used to it. Her brain understands the message from her ear and so she does not lose her balance.

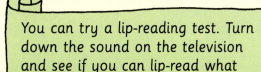

When hearing does not work

People who cannot hear make extra use of their sense of sight. Many deaf people understand what other people are saying by lip-reading and by watching their hands. They also might be able to 'read' sign language.

You can try a lip-reading test. Turn down the sound on the television and see if you can lip-read what people are saying.

Can you find other ways to help deaf people 'hear'?

More about: brain pp5, 6, 12 nerves p26 senses pp22–25

Sight

Look at your eyes in a mirror. What can you see?

Your eyes are very delicate. Dust and dirt can scratch them. Fumes can make them sore. Bright light can damage them. That is why you should never look directly at the Sun.

pupil
a hole which changes in size. On a bright day, the hole gets smaller so that you are not dazzled by too much light. When it is dark, your pupils get bigger to allow more light into your eye

eyelids
wipe away bits of dirt and dust and protect your eyes while you are asleep

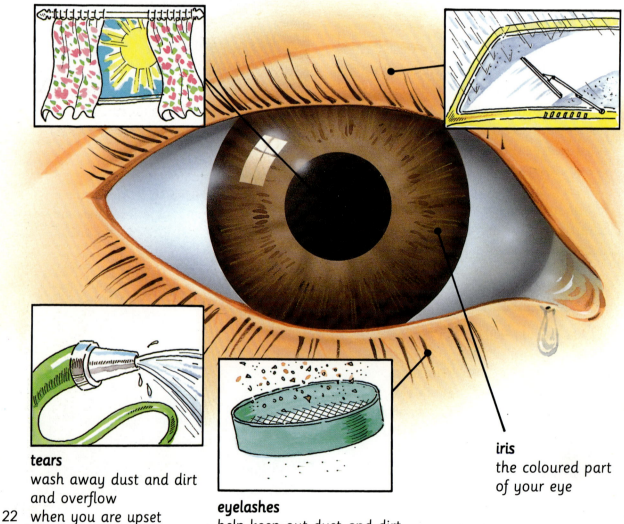

tears
wash away dust and dirt and overflow when you are upset

eyelashes
help keep out dust and dirt

iris
the coloured part of your eye

How you see

When you look at something, light bounces off it. The light passes into your eyes in straight lines through your pupils. A picture is formed upside-down at the back of each eye. Messages about the picture pass to your brain and it turns the picture the right way up. A newborn baby's brain has not learnt to do this. The baby sees everything upside-down!

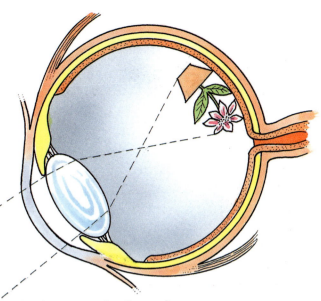

When sight does not work

People who cannot see make extra use of their sense of touch. Blind people tell what other people look like by feeling the shapes of their faces. They often have a better sense of hearing, too.

Blind people read books written in braille, a special alphabet. This was invented by a Frenchman called Louis Braille. Can you find out more about Louis Braille and his alphabet?

More about: brain pp5, 6, 12   hearing pp20–21   touch p25

Taste and smell

You taste with your tongue, but smell helps you to recognise tastes. If you have a cold, you cannot taste your food very well. That is because you cannot smell it.

Nerves take smell messages to your brain.

Behind your nose is a large space which has a special lining. In the lining there are nerves which pick up smells.

When you breathe in, air passes into your nose.

Different parts of your tongue recognise different tastes.

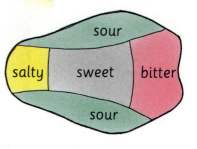

Touch

Your sense of touch helps you to recognise things. You can feel if things are hard or soft, rough or smooth, hot or cold.

Touch helps you **communicate** thoughts and feelings to other people. What examples can you think of?

Danger signals

Our senses help us recognise danger. We usually can hear traffic coming towards us, even if we cannot see it. Red and orange are colours which can warn us of danger.

Poisonous foods such as berries, often have bright colours or a bitter taste which warns us not to swallow them. We can taste when food has gone bad. It would make us ill if we ate it.

Smell warns us of danger, too. You can smell smoke from a fire. Bad food smells unpleasant. You can feel pain. This warns you about illness or danger.

You use your senses all the time. They tell you what is happening around you. You rely on them to warn you of danger.

Do you think you use some senses more than others?

Which senses are you using now?

More about: breathing pp14–15 food pp34–37 senses pp20–23

Your skin and hair

Your skin holds your body together and protects everything inside. It stops water and harmful germs getting into your body. Your skin also helps to control your body's temperature.

Your skin is covered with fine hairs. It contains sweat **glands** and special nerves. Some feel heat, cold and pain. Others can tell whether things are rough or smooth, hard or soft.

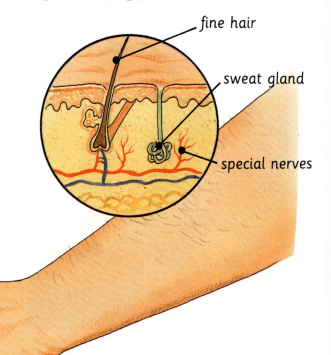

Hair

Each hair on your head grows for five or six years and then drops out. A new hair grows in its place.

Why do some people have curly hair? Each hair grows out of a thin tube in the skin. If the tube is round, the hair grows straight. If it is oval, the hair is curly.

Skin colour

Your skin protects your body from harmful sun rays. People in hot countries need more protection than people in colder countries. This is why their skin is darker.

If fair-skinned people stay out in the sun, their skin turns a darker colour. This suntan fades after a while. If they sunbathe for too long, their skin burns.

Nails

Your nails protect your fingers and toes. They are made of a special extra hard substance.

Did you know...?

- Most people have about 100 000 hairs on their head. Each hair grows about 0·3 mm every day. That means all your hair added together grows 30 000 mm (30 m) every day!

- The longest nails were grown by a Chinese priest. They measured 58 cm.

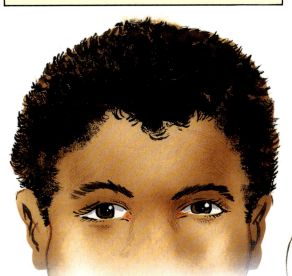

More about: hair pp40, 54 skin pp28, 40 temperature pp28-29

Natural reactions

In hot weather, your sweat glands pour out a clear, salty liquid. This cools your body. Blood flows near the surface of your skin to lose heat so your face might look red.

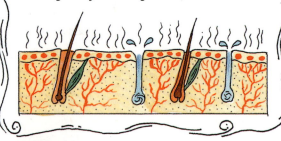

The right temperature

Sometimes the temperature is hot outside, sometimes it is cold. But the temperature inside your body stays the same most of the time. Your body **adapts** to hot or cold weather.

Do you ever get 'goose pimples' when it is cold? The hairs on your skin stand upright. Warm air is trapped between them, keeping you warmer. When you shiver, your muscles twitch quickly. This movement also helps you warm up.

Sometimes your body cannot adapt. If you are ill, it may not be able to cool you down. Your temperature goes up and you feel very hot.

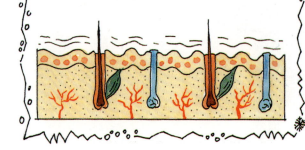

If the weather is very cold, goose pimples and shivering cannot help enough. Your temperature drops. Then you need to wrap up in warm clothes.

Fight or flight?

Do you want to fight or run away when something frightens you? This feeling protects you. Your senses recognise danger and pass messages to your brain. A special substance called **adrenalin** makes your body work harder to escape the danger.

Quick action

If you touch something hot, the pain makes you draw back your hand immediately. You do not have to think about it. It is a **reflex action**.

Sometimes you have to react quickly to avoid an accident.

Imagine you are riding your bike.

Suddenly you see danger ahead.

Your brain sends a message to your muscles and you jam on the brakes.

The time between seeing the danger and braking is called **reaction time**.

Never run suddenly into the road! A car driver might not react quickly enough to avoid you.

More about: brain pp5, 6, 12 senses pp20–25 muscles pp12–13

Staying healthy

Your body will not stay fit and healthy unless you look after it. If you are not healthy, it does not mean you are ill. It means your body is not as fit as it should be. How fit are you? Your body needs four things to keep healthy.

good diet
Eat proper meals but not too many fattening foods.

regular exercise
During exercise, your heart, lungs and muscles are working extra hard.

fresh air
Important, especially as air in towns is often spoilt or **polluted**.

sleep and relaxation
You need time to rest and recover after work and exercise.

Why do you need water?

Your body is nearly three-quarters water. It is in your blood. Your brain is nearly all water! You are losing water all the time. How do you think this happens? You have to drink more water to replace it.

How your body protects you

Your skin keeps germs out, but they can get in through a cut or wound. Wash cuts carefully and cover with a plaster.

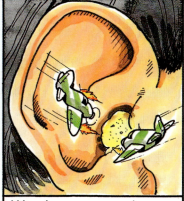

Wax in your ears traps dirt.

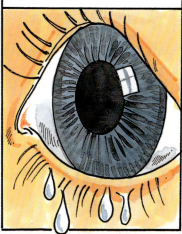

Tears wash dust out of your eyes.

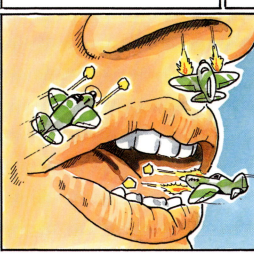

Mucus in your nose and throat traps germs, dust and dirt. You feel a tickle and cough or sneeze to get rid of them. Germs which are not trapped in your throat are often killed off by juices in your stomach and intestines.

If germs avoid all this protection, your white blood cells attack them.

What causes illness?

Do you sometimes get colds? Colds are caused by germs which attack your body.

Sometimes there are so many germs that your body cannot stop them all. If someone near you has a cold and sneezes, millions of germs pass into the air. You cannot help breathing them in and you catch the cold.

Keep fit!

Your body cannot stop germs so well if you do not keep yourself healthy. If you do not eat the right foods or take enough exercise, your body weakens. It finds it difficult to fight off germs and you become ill more easily.

More about: diet pp34-35 germs pp17, 26 pollution p43

Helping your body fight back

Sometimes your body needs help to fight off illness. Scientists have found cures for many diseases. These are called medicines or **drugs**.

Some medicines can be bought at a chemist's shop. They are usually for things like headaches or sore throats. Your doctor may give you a **prescription** for other medicines. The doctor decides what and how much you should take.

Harmful drugs

Medicines are safe if you take the right amount. Taking too much is dangerous and can kill you. Some drugs are not medicines. People take these drugs because they make them feel good. But this feeling does not last, so they take more. Soon they cannot do without them.

Never take drugs unless your parents or a doctor are there to check they are suitable and will not harm you.

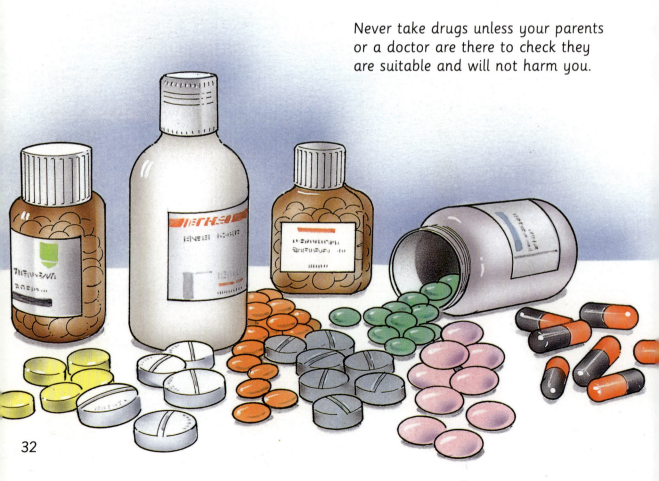

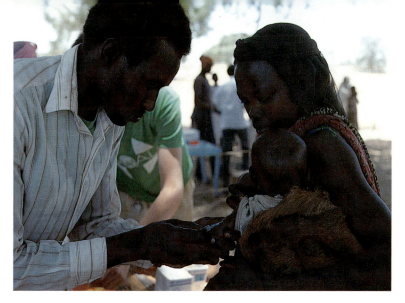

Antibiotics and other medicines can be given to people as injections. When you were a baby, you probably had injections to stop you catching diseases such as measles and tetanus.

Penicillin

Has your doctor ever given you **antibiotics**? They attack germs but do not harm your body's cells. **Penicillin** was the first antibiotic. It was discovered in 1928 by Alexander Fleming.

In this picture, two **bacteria** have been coloured and made much bigger so that you can see them. The one at the top has been destroyed by an antibiotic.

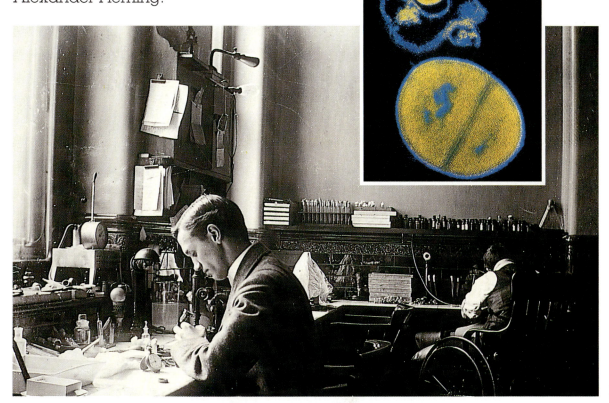

More about: cells pp9, 48   doctors pp52–53   germs pp17, 26, 31

A healthy diet

Your body needs food to live and grow, but why does it matter what *sort* of food you eat?

Food is made up of different parts – **carbohydrate**, **protein**, **fat**, **fibre**, **vitamins**, and **minerals**. These are all necessary to keep you healthy. No single food contains everything you need. So you have to eat a balanced mixture of foods.

Choosing good food

A few years ago, most people ate white bread. This is made from flour which has been **processed**. Flour is made by crushing brown wheat grains to a powder. Parts of the grain are removed to make the flour smooth and white. But, these parts provide fibre, vitamins and minerals. Many people now choose to eat wholewheat bread because it is better for them.

A balanced diet includes

Many foods are processed in factories. Processing can remove some of the natural goodness of the food.

minerals such as calcium for strong, healthy teeth and bones

protein for growth

vitamins for healthy skin and body

fibre to help push waste materials through your gut

foods to fill you up

fibre

carbohydrates, including sugar and starch, for energy

protein to help you grow and repair your body

foods stored as body fat which helps to keep your body warm and can be used for energy

More about: bones pp8–11   food pp36–37   muscles pp12–13

Energy

If you eat too many energy foods, you will not be able to run faster. Your body only uses what it needs. It stores the rest as fat and you put on weight.

Someone doing heavy work or taking a lot of exercise uses more energy than someone who sits at a desk. He or she will burn up more energy foods before getting fat. Energy is measured in **kilojoules** (kJ).

Did you know...?

A person sitting at a desk uses up about 320 kJ an hour. You would get this amount of energy from three lumps of sugar.

The chocolate test

14 minutes

24 minutes

52 minutes

4 hours

5 hours

How long does it take you to burn off a bar of chocolate (1100 kJ)?

What happens if you have a bad diet?

Some food has hardly any goodness. It is called 'junk' food because it fills you up but it does not keep you healthy.

Food for health

If you do not eat enough vitamins and minerals, your body cannot grow properly. It is not fit enough to fight off illnesses.

If children have too few vitamins and minerals in their diet, they can get bone diseases such as rickets. Their bones do not grow straight.

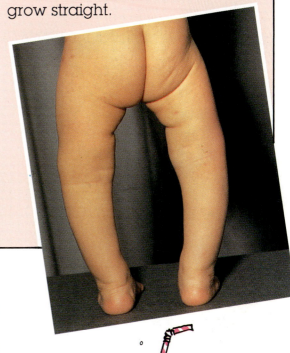

More about: diet pp34–35   energy pp7, 18   exercise pp38–39

Taking exercise

Exercise is good for you and helps your body in three ways.

Stamina
Having **stamina** means that you can exercise for a long time without getting tired. Building up stamina strengthens your heart and lungs. Jogging builds up stamina. As you improve, you can run longer distances.

Strength
Exercising with weights is good for strength. It builds up the muscles.

Suppleness
If you are **supple**, you can bend easily. Bending and stretching exercises make you supple.

Feel your heartbeat

You can feel your heartbeat at a special place on your wrist. This is called your **pulse**. Can you find your pulse at any other places on your body?

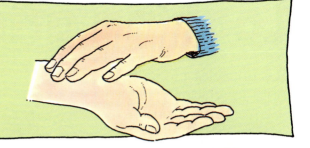

When you exercise, you breathe more deeply and take extra oxygen into your lungs. Your heart works harder to pump the oxygen to your muscles. Exercise strengthens the heart and lungs. Muscles become stronger as they get used to exercise. Your joints move more easily and do not become stiff.

Most young children get enough exercise by running and playing. Older children and adults need to plan their exercise. They should exercise two or three times a week.

You should put on warm clothes after exercise because your body soon cools once you stop.

Swimming is the best all-round exercise.

More about: exercise pp30, 50 heart pp16–17 lungs pp14–15

Looking after your body

It is important to look after the outside of your body. This is called personal **hygiene**.

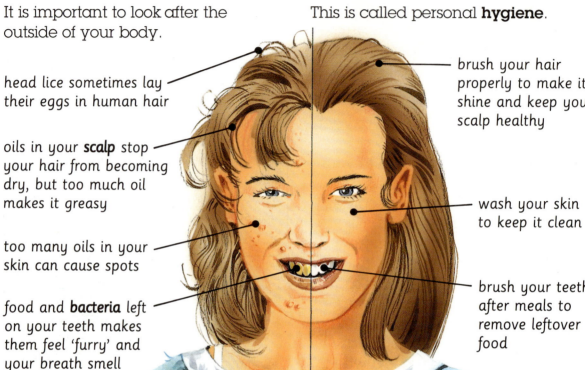

- head lice sometimes lay their eggs in human hair
- oils in your **scalp** stop your hair from becoming dry, but too much oil makes it greasy
- too many oils in your skin can cause spots
- food and **bacteria** left on your teeth makes them feel 'furry' and your breath smell
- dried sweat smells unpleasant
- brush your hair properly to make it shine and keep your scalp healthy
- wash your skin to keep it clean
- brush your teeth after meals to remove leftover food
- wash your clothes regularly

Going to the dentist

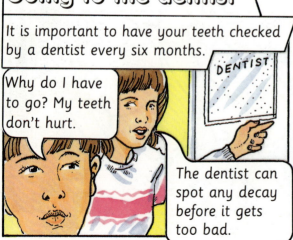

It is important to have your teeth checked by a dentist every six months.

"Why do I have to go? My teeth don't hurt."

The dentist can spot any decay before it gets too bad.

"There is some decay in one tooth. I'll have to **drill** it away and fill the hole with a special mixture."

Did you know...?

You have 20 baby teeth which start to drop out when you are five. New adult teeth grow. Adults have 32 teeth. Your adult teeth have to last you for the rest of your life. That is why it is important to look after them.

Your teeth have different jobs to do. This is an adult's bottom jaw. The top jaw has the same number of teeth.

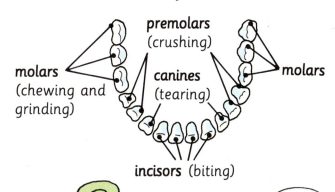

premolars (crushing)
molars (chewing and grinding)
canines (tearing)
molars
incisors (biting)

Looking after your teeth

Always brush your teeth thoroughly after meals. Too many sweets and sugary foods can cause **decay.**

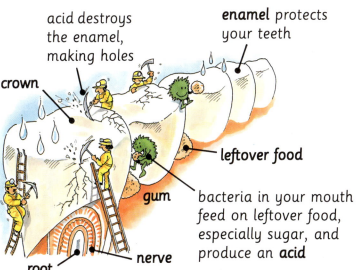

acid destroys the enamel, making holes

enamel protects your teeth

crown

leftover food

gum

bacteria in your mouth feed on leftover food, especially sugar, and produce an **acid**

root

nerve

The tooth test

Eggshells are made of material like your teeth. To see what acid does to your teeth, put pieces of eggshell into two cups. Cover one shell with water. Cover the other with vinegar, an acid. When all the liquid has disappeared, what do you notice?

The fillings will set hard like the tooth itself.

But try not to bite on it for a few hours.

Your teeth are growing properly. Your mouth and gums are healthy. But you must cut down on sweets if you don't want another filling!

Can I have a yellow badge next time, please?

More about: hair p26 skin pp26–28 sweat p28

Dangers to your body

Many things can harm your body. There are dangers like fires and road accidents, which can wound or kill people. Other things harm your body more gradually.

Smoking

Smoking damages the lungs and can cause diseases like lung cancer. Smoking has other **side effects**. Tobacco contains a drug called **nicotine**. Nicotine makes the heart beat faster. This puts a strain on the heart causing heart disease.

Too much fat

Eating too many fatty foods can cause heart disease. Fats clog up the arteries so that blood cannot flow through them properly.

Alcohol

Drinks such as wine and beer contain **alcohol**. Alcohol can be pleasant in small quantities but it is a drug. People can become **addicted** to alcohol. Too much alcohol damages the liver.

Pollution

Breathing in dirty, polluted air harms your lungs and causes lung diseases. At one time, the smoke from factories made the air filthy in many towns and cities. Then, laws were passed to stop this type of air pollution.

A greater problem is pollution from car exhaust fumes. The lead in petrol is harmful, so lead-free petrol is on sale now.

More about: diet pp34–37 drugs pp32–33 pollution p30

Rest and relaxation

It is important to relax after exercise. Sitting down is not enough. You have to make every part of your body rest.

Stress

If you are worried about something or you cannot relax, you can get a condition called **stress**.

People under stress cannot sleep or eat well, so they become tired and run-down. This makes the stress worse. People have to learn to relax properly before they can get over stress. It also helps to talk about worries with someone.

The importance of sleep

Most people need about eight hours' sleep. Children need more than adults because they are growing.

When you are asleep, your heart beats more slowly. Your muscles rest. You can forget any worries. Your mind and body are resting and preparing for the next day.

Dreaming

Most people have four or five dreams each night. Everybody dreams, although some people do not remember their dreams. Your dreams probably don't make sense. Many people think that dreams are the brain's way of sorting out things that happened in the past.

More about: brain pp5, 6, 12   exercise pp38–39   relaxation p30

The human cycle

Living things are changing all the time. They are born, they grow older and, in the end, they die. During their lifetime, living things can **reproduce**. They produce young which are like them. Think what would happen if they could not do this.

Growing older

A baby grows into a child and the child grows into an adult. An adult man and woman can produce more babies, and so the human cycle continues.

As people grow older, their muscles begin to lose their strength. Their joints become stiff. They do things more slowly. Their skin wrinkles. Older people sometimes become forgetful. They may not be able to hear or see as well. An older person's body picks up illnesses more easily.

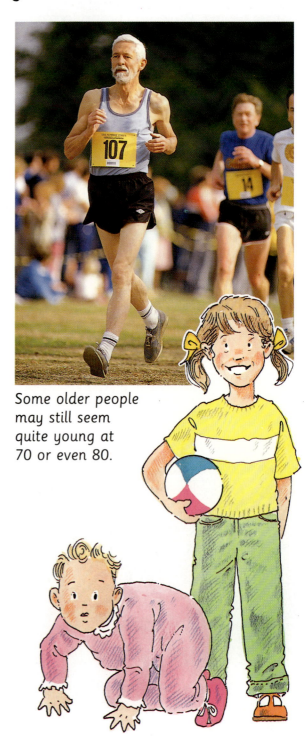

Some older people may still seem quite young at 70 or even 80.

Did you know...?

The most common cause of death in Europe, North America and Australia is heart disease.

When someone dies

When your body has grown too old, tired or ill to cope with life, you stop breathing and your heart stops beating. We might feel very sad when someone dies because we will miss seeing them and talking to them. But it is a part of the life cycle.

Did you know...?

People have been known to live as long as 120 years.

More about: babies pp48–59 growing older pp60–61 illness p31–33

A new life

A baby grows inside a woman's body but it is made by a man and a woman together. A woman's body produces tiny eggs. If an egg joins with a **sperm** from a man's body, a new life can begin. We say that the egg has been **fertilised**.

The pregnant mother

A woman who is expecting a baby is **pregnant**. Pregnancy lasts about nine months while the baby grows in her **womb**. Its food and oxygen come from her body. She may feel unwell during the first few weeks of pregnancy. This is because her body is getting used to having a baby growing inside her.

How does a tiny egg become a baby?

This drawing shows a sperm fertilising an egg. After the egg has been fertilised, it splits into two, then into four, then into eight.

Where does the egg come from?

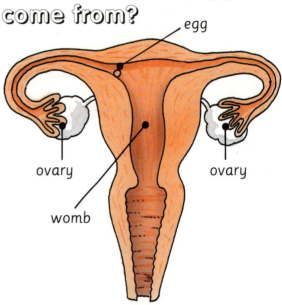

Every month, an egg travels from one of a woman's **ovaries** to her womb. If the egg is not fertilised, it dies after two days. If it is fertilised, it develops in her womb.

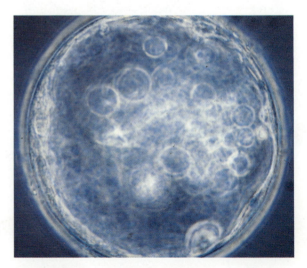

1 week
The fertilised egg goes on splitting until a small group of cells has formed. This cluster buries itself in the side of the womb. The cells continue to multiply quickly.

Did you know...?

- A baby Indian elephant has to wait about 23 months to be born.
- A baby American opossum has to wait only 12 days.

The baby's lifeline

As the baby grows, the mother's womb stretches to make room for it. The baby is surrounded by a bag of liquid protecting it from knocks and bumps.

At first, the baby gets food from the womb. But during the first weeks of pregnancy, a special organ called the **placenta** forms. The baby is joined to the placenta by the **umbilical cord**.

How the placenta works

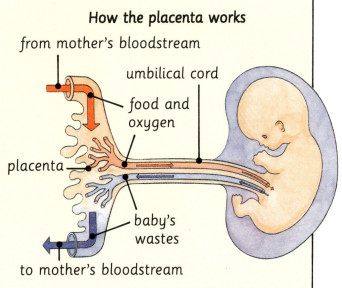

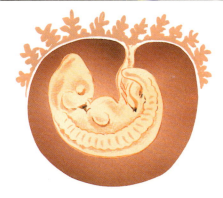

4 weeks
The baby is about 6 mm long. It has a head and brain, and its heart is beating.

9 weeks
The baby looks like a tiny person with arms and legs. Its organs have formed, and so have its eyes and ears.

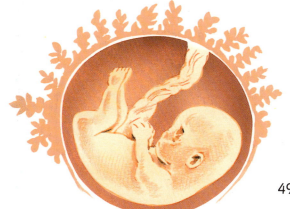

More about: babies pp50–53, 56–59   growth pp35, 60–61   oxygen p14

Preparing for the birth

The mother's body changes a lot during pregnancy. Her breasts begin to produce milk to feed the baby when it is born. Her body swells as her womb stretches to let the baby grow. She must look after herself and rest as much as possible, especially during the last few weeks.

The developing baby takes food from its mother, so she should keep to a healthy diet. Smoking, drinking alcohol or taking drugs during pregnancy can harm the baby.

Strong muscles push the baby out when it is born. Exercises help to strengthen these muscles. Many women go to special exercise classes to prepare for the birth.

The story continues

5 months

The mother's tummy looks quite big. She can feel her baby moving as it stretches its legs or turns round. It feels like a bird fluttering inside her.

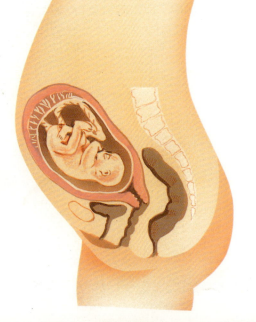

7 months

She can see her baby's movements quite clearly as it kicks against her stomach.

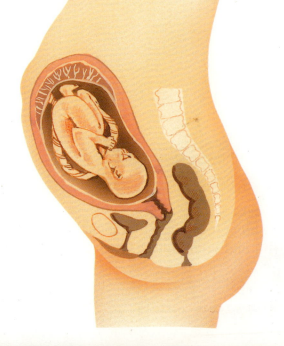

9 months

The baby does not have room to move much. It turns itself round so that its head is facing the opening of the womb. The baby weighs between 2·5 and 4·5 kg. It is fully developed and ready to be born.

Did you know...?

- Most women give birth to only one baby at the end of their pregnancy. But, the largest ever-recorded number of babies born at one time was nine!

- The tailless tenrec holds the record for mammals with 31 babies born at one time.

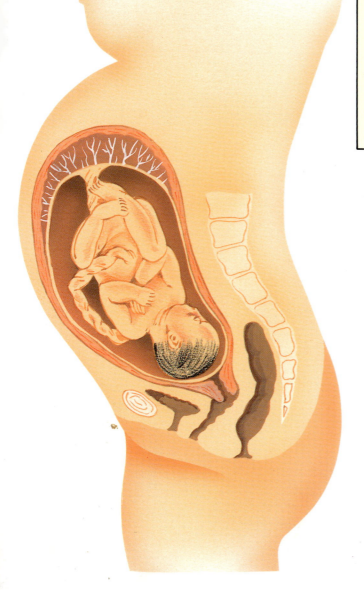

More about: babies pp48–49, 52–53   diet pp34–37   exercise pp38–39

The baby is born

When the baby is ready to be born, the muscles of the womb start to push it out. The mother feels sharp pains. This tells her that her baby will arrive soon.

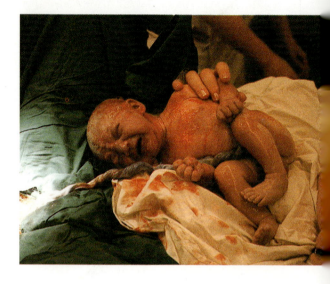

When the baby is born, it is still attached to the mother by the umbilical cord. The cord is cut by a doctor or a **midwife**. Your tummy button is the place where you were joined to your mother when you were in her womb.

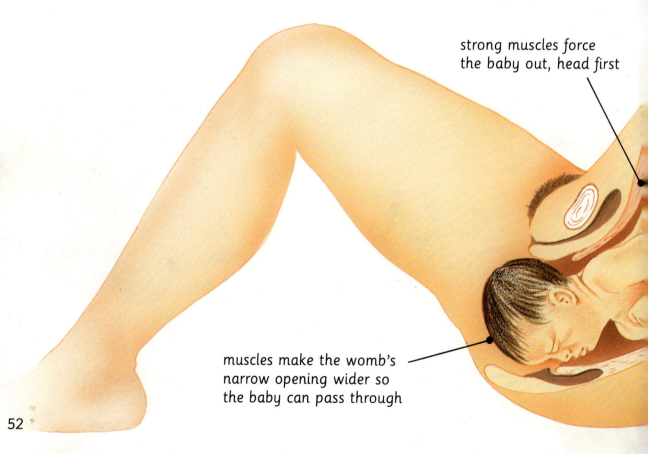

strong muscles force the baby out, head first

muscles make the womb's narrow opening wider so the baby can pass through

In hospital

Most women have their babies in hospital. When the pains come more often, the mother knows that it is time to go into hospital. It still may be some hours before her baby is born.

Doctors and nurses help her. When the baby is born, it is given straight to its happy mother to hold for the first time. She has used a lot of energy having her baby. Now she needs time to recover.

The baby is tiny and delicate. Nurses show the mother how to bath it and change its nappy. Doctors check that both mother and baby are fit and well before they leave hospital.

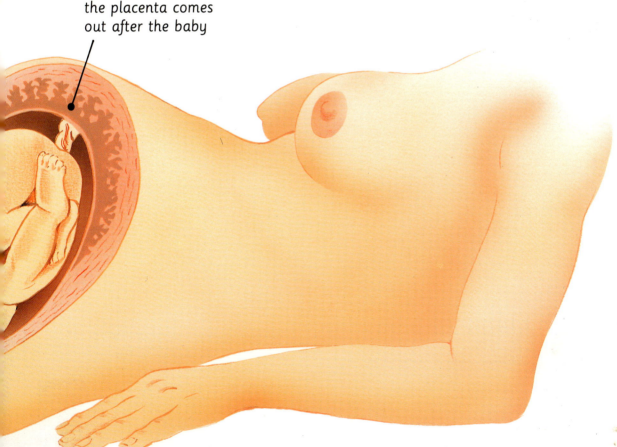

the placenta comes out after the baby

More about: babies pp48–51, 56–59   placenta p49   womb pp48–51

Who do you look like?

You may look like your mother or your father, but you do not look *exactly* the same as either of them.

The egg and the sperm which form a baby both contain sets of instructions called **genes.** These instructions affect what the baby will look like. Everything about the way you look is **inherited** through your parents. This includes the colour of your hair and eyes, how tall you are, the colour of your skin, and, of course, whether you are a girl or a boy.

Each sperm and egg contain slightly different instructions. That is why no two people look the same.

Identical twins

The only people who look almost exactly like each other are identical twins.

Identical twins are born when the mother's egg divides into two separate parts after it has been fertilised. Two babies develop from the same egg.

Fingerprints

Look at the tips of your fingers. Can you see a pattern on the skin? Fingerprints are caused by bumps and ridges on your skin.

No two people in the world have the same fingerprints, not even identical twins. The police use fingerprints to **identify** people. People can disguise themselves but they cannot disguise their fingerprints.

Where you live

The people you meet and the **environment** or surroundings you live in also affect you. As you grow up, you form your own ideas and develop your own **personality**. You learn new things about the world around you. This helps to decide what you will be like as an adult.

All these people are members of the same family. How many likenesses can you see? Which two people are the most alike?

More about: developing egg p48   learning pp56–59   skin pp26–28

A baby's first year

Having a baby changes the parents' lives. New-born babies cannot do much for themselves. They cry when they are hungry or uncomfortable. They are comforted by warmth and cuddling. They can taste and smell, but cannot see clearly. They cannot **focus** their eyes. They can hear but they do not know what the sounds mean. They know nothing about the world around them.

A baby in the house

Parents have to think about their baby's safety. Babies put things in their mouth so they should not have toys with sharp edges or with small parts that come off.

As their baby learns to crawl and walk, stairs, fires and hot pans in the kitchen can be dangerous. Parents must make sure that the baby cannot run into the road. As children grow older, they are taught to recognise dangers for themselves.

A baby learns a lot in the first year

by 3 months

clutches rattle

moves head to look at things

makes noises

smiles at people

by 6 months

can sit up if propped against something

turns head towards noises

focusses eyes

can hold a cup

laughs

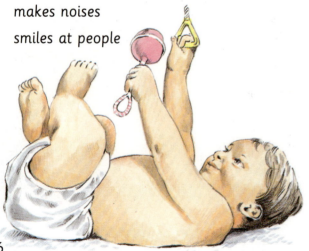

Looking after a new baby

The first few weeks of a baby's life are very busy for the parents. The baby has to be fed often. Most babies wake every two or three hours for food. Many mothers breast-feed their baby. Some babies have special milk from a bottle, then other people can feed them, too.

Babies spend a lot of time asleep. They must be kept warm but not too hot. They also need fresh air.

Babies should be bathed and have their hair washed every day. Bathing a tiny baby is tricky. The baby has to be held carefully all the time.

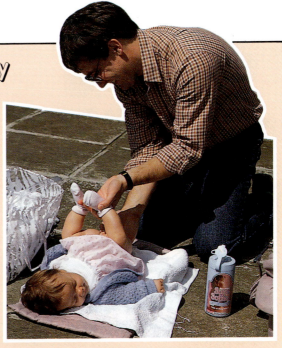

It is important to keep babies clean. Nappies must be changed when they are wet or dirty.

by 9 months

crawls

can stand if holding on to something

makes a variety of different noises

by 1 year

starts to walk

can understand quite a few words

plays with toys such as stacking bricks

drinks from a cup

may be able to say two or three words

More about: growing older pp46, 60–61 hygiene p40 senses pp20–25

Learning about the world

Babies start to learn about the world by touching things around them. They touch their parents' faces to get to know them better. They learn how different objects feel by picking them up and sucking them.

The time parents spend with their baby is important. Babies learn things from looking at books and playing games. This helps them talk and recognise the things they see. They also learn that they are safe at home and that their parents will look after them.

Your memory

You could not learn anything if you did not have a memory. Every time you learn something new, your memory stores it away for later. When you were a baby, your memory stored away information about new things. You could recognise those things when you saw them again. Later, when you learnt to read, your memory stored away that information, too.

Learning to talk

New-born babies can make sounds but they have to learn to talk. They listen to people around them and copy the sounds they make. First, they say single words like "No", "Mama", "Dadda". Next, they put two or three words together. Then, they say whole sentences that people can understand. By the time they are three or four, they have learnt a range of words which help them describe things.

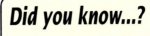

Did you know...? Crows can be taught to say more than 150 words.

Babies are curious about things around them. This helps them learn. They try out things for themselves — what floats in the bath, what bounces, why do objects feel different? As children grow, they work out things for themselves. They learn to think hard about questions and problems, and try to find the answers.

Understanding

Your memory stores facts, but how do you learn to understand them? Babies often cry when their mother goes out because they think she has gone away for ever. They do not understand that she will be back later. Gradually, they learn from **experience** that when their mother goes out she will come back.

More about: brain pp5, 6, 12 talking pp14–15 touch p25

The child grows up

Children learn at different speeds. They also grow at different speeds. You may grow quickly for a while, so that you are taller than other people in your class. Then you stop growing for a bit and other people catch up. You will still end up the height you are meant to be.

People stop growing when they are 17 or 18. By this time, their bodies have changed. They have become adult men and women who can produce children of their own.

Making friends

As you grow up, you meet a lot of other people. You like some better than others. These people may become your friends.

Friends are important. You can do things together and share interests with each other. You can tell them about things that worry you and help them if they are worried or in trouble.

Making friends is not easy. You have to think about other people and take an interest in them. As they grow up, children get better at this. They learn how to play with other children. Then they choose their friends.

Key words

The meanings of words can depend on how and when they are used. You may find that as you learn more about science the meanings change slightly.

acid a sharp, sour-tasting substance; vinegar and lemon juice contain acids

adapt change to suit the environment

addicted feel you cannot do without something such as alcohol or cigarettes

adrenalin a substance that helps the body react quickly to danger

alcohol a substance in drinks such as wine and beer

antibiotics drugs that kill bacteria but do not harm body cells

arteries tubes in the body which carry blood away from the heart

bacteria very tiny living things which are all around us; some cause disease

bladder a bag in which waste liquid collects before passing out of the body

carbohydrates a food which provides energy such as sugar, bread and potatoes

carbon dioxide one of the gases in air

cartilage tough, rubbery material which protects the ends of bones

cells the tiny 'building blocks' which make up our bodies

circulation the journey of the blood round the body

clot the joining together of parts of a liquid so that it stops flowing

communicate give and receive information

cramp sudden tightening of the muscles

decay to rot

diet the different foods you eat

digestion preparing the food you have eaten for your body to use

disease an illness, usually caused by germs in the body

dissolve become part of a solution

drill to bore a hole with a pointed tool

drug something which changes the way the body works, such as medicines, tobacco and alcohol

enamel hard, smooth coating on teeth

energy the power to work

environment surroundings

experience knowledge gained by doing and seeing things

fat substance which the body needs to stay healthy; found in cooking oils, dairy products and meat

fertilise to join an egg with a sperm so that a baby grows

fibre foods which have a rough texture

focus see an object clearly

fuel a material which burns to make things work

gas a substance which you cannot see: air is made up of gases

genes tiny parts of each cell which tell every part of the body how it will grow

germs tiny living things that cause illness

gland an organ which gives out fluid

gums the flesh around the bottom of the teeth covering the roots

hygiene cleanliness

identify find out who a person is or what an object is

inherited passed on from person to person

kidneys the organs which help to filter or 'clean' the blood

kilojoule unit of measurement of heat

large intestine tube where solid waste from food collects and is forced out of the body

ligament tough bands which hold the joints in place

liver organ which sorts the food for the body to use

mammal warm-blooded animal covered with hair which has a backbone; most give birth to live young and produce milk to feed them

marrow soft substance at the centre of a bone where blood cells are made

midwife a nurse who is specially trained to help women who are having babies

minerals a natural substance which is not an animal or plant, such as rocks and metals

mucus jelly-like substance which coats and protects organs

nerve a pathway made of a thin thread or bundles of thread, which passes messages to and from the brain

nicotine harmful substance in tobacco; people become addicted to nicotine

organ a part of the body which has a special job such as the brain or stomach

ovaries the organs in a woman's body where eggs are produced

oxygen one of the gases in air

penicillin antibiotic discovered by Alexander Fleming in 1928

personality what a person is like

placenta the organ in the womb through which food and oxygen are passed from a mother to her baby

poisonous a substance which could make you very ill

polluted spoiled or made dirty

pregnant carrying a baby in the womb

prescription written order for medicine given by a doctor

processed treated in a factory

protein a substance found in some foods such as meat and eggs which is used for growth and repair

pulse a place where you can feel blood throbbing through an artery

reaction time the time it takes for your eyes and ears to send a message to your brain and your brain to act on it

reflex action automatic action you do not have to think about

relaxation allowing all the muscles to go limp so that your body rests

reproduce produce young

reptile an animal with a scaly skin whose body temperature changes with its surroundings such as a snake or tortoise

saliva the liquid in the mouth

scalp skin and hair on top of the head

side effects unexpected things which happen as a result of doing something

small intestine tube where food is finally broken up and dissolved

sprain to twist or tear a muscle

sperm reproduction cells which are produced in a man's body

stamina you have stamina if you can do something, such as running, for a long time

stress a feeling of strain and worry

suppleness you are supple if you can bend parts of your body easily

temperature the amount of heat in something measured with a thermometer

tendon a group of fibres which attaches a muscle to a bone

transplant to replace a diseased organ with a healthy organ from another person

umbilical cord attaches the baby to the placenta in the mother's womb

urine waste water that passes out of the body through the bladder

vein a tube carrying blood to the heart

vibrate move backwards and forwards very quickly

vitamins substances, found in foods such as fruit and vegetables, which are essential for good health

vocal cords two thin bands in the throat which vibrate when air passes over them making sounds

windpipe tube which joins the mouth to the lungs

womb organ in a woman's body where a baby grows, also known as the uterus

Index

adrenalin 29
alcohol 42
antibiotics 33
appearance 5, 54–5

babies 4, 46–59
bacteria 33, 40
birth 46, 48–53
bladder 18
blindness 23
blood 7, 9, 16–17, 19, 28
bones 6, 8–12
braille 23
brain 5, 6, 12, 24, 29, 45
breathing 14–15, 24, 39
bruises 17

cells 9, 17
circulation 16
colds 31
cramp 13

deafness 21
death 47
dentist 40–1
diet 30, 34–5, 37
digestion 18–19
disease 32–3, 40
dizziness 21
dreaming 45
drugs 32–3

ears 6, 20–1, 31
energy 7, 36
environment 55
eyes 6, 22–3, 31
exercise 30, 38–9

family 5, 54–5
fingerprints 55
fitness 31
food 7, 16, 18–19, 25, 34–5, 37, 40
fresh air 30
friendship 60

genes 54–5
germs 17, 31
growth 37, 49, 56–61

hair 26–7, 28, 40
head lice 40
health 30–1, 34–5, 37
hearing 20–1
heart 6, 8, 16–17, 39, 42
hygiene 40–1

illness 32–3
injections 33
intestines 18–19

joints 8, 10–11

kidneys 6, 18

language 5, 59
learning 55–61
life cycle 46–7
liver 6
lungs 8, 14–15, 39

mammals 4
medicine 32–3
memory 58
movement 10, 12–13
muscles 7, 12–13, 18, 39

nails 27
nerves 24, 26
nose 24

old age 47, 61
organs 6

penicillin 33
personality 55
pollution 43
pregnancy 48–51
pulse 39

reactions 28–9
recognition 58
reflex action 29
relaxation 30, 44–5
reproduction 46, 48
rest 44–5

saliva 18
senses 20–5
sight 22–3
skeleton 8
skin 26–7, 31, 40
sleep 30, 44–5
smell 24–5
smoking 42
spots 40
sprains 13
stomach 19, 31
stress 44–5
sweating 26, 28, 40

talking 15, 59
taste 24–5
teeth 18, 40–1
temperature 4, 26, 28
tongue 24
touch 25, 58
twins 5, 54

understanding 59

vocal cords 15

washing 40
windpipe 14
wounds 17, 31